KOKORO

THE NEW JERUSALEM
& THE RISE OF THE TRUE HUMAN BEING

An Illustrated Story by
Neil Hague

Quester

First published in 2009 by
Quester Publications

Hard back vesrion published in 2015

Copyright © 2015 Neil Hague
All rights reserved
www.neilhague.com

No part of this book may be reproduced in any form
without permission from the publisher, except for quotation of
brief passages in criticism

Cover Design: Neil Hague

British Library Cataloguing-in Publication Data
A catalogue record for this book is
available from the British Library

ISBN 0-9541904-8-4

Printed by Lightning Source

*I dedicate this book to world peace.
Know that all peace comes from within.*

"Love seeketh not itself to please, nor for itself hath any care, but for another gives its ease, and builds a Heaven in Hell's despair."
William Blake

"All that we are is the result of what we have thought."
Buddha

"Our greatest glory is not in never falling but in rising every time we fall."
Confucius

"Set me like a seal upon thy heart, love is as strong as death."
Song of Solomon 8:6

"We who lived in concentration camps can remember the men who walked through the huts comforting others, giving away their last piece of bread. They may have been few in number, but they offer sufficient proof that everything can be taken from a man but one thing: the last of the human freedoms—to choose one's attitude in any given set of circumstances, to choose one's own way."
Viktor Frankl

In the reality of many realities, how we see what we see affects the quality of our reality. We are children of earth and sky, DNA descendant and ancestor, humanbeing, physical spirit bone flesh blood as spirit.

We are in time and space but we're from beyond time and space. The past is part of the present, the future part of the present life and being are interwoven.

We are DNA of Earth, Moon, Planets, Stars. We are related to the universal Creator created creation, spirit and intelligence with clarity, being human as power.

We are a part of the memories of evolution, these memories carry knowledge, these memories carry our identity beneath race, gender, class, age beneath citizen, business, state, religion.

We are human being and these memories are trying to remind us, human beings, humanbeings, it is time to rise up, remember who you are.

John Trudell
(American Indian musician, poet and actor)

Act One: Alpha

"Just as there was only one at the beginning, so too in this work everything comes from One and returns to One."

Synesios
4th Century Greek Alchemist.

Consider the birds of the air, they neither sow nor reap nor gather into barns, and yet your Father feeds them. Are you not of more value than they?"

Jesus Christ *(Matt. 6:26)*

Somewhere in the timeless ocean of consciousness, an all-encompassing love simultaneously imagined itself into infinite realities. This love was-called the *One* and it was the very fabric of the water that brings the ocean into existence. In every life that is born the *One* exists and in every heart it dwells. The *One* exists within every living form - both seen and unseen. It is in all sounds, colours, shapes and forces that exist. It encompasses both light and dark, silence and noise and there was no place or smallest particle that was not part of this divine ocean of *Oneness*.

In the darkest recesses of silence a spark of inspiration ignited in the mind of infinite awareness and instantly, at the speed of thought, all life came into existence. Just as many thoughts occur in our own minds the *One* imagined infinite realities, possibilities and worlds. Many of these realities became visible and others remained as ideas - invisible to the life forms taking shape in the mind of the *One*. In an instant all that was once silent now sang to the sound of life, vibrating, orbiting and cycling. Everything now vibrated and danced around the centre to the tune that inspired it. The dancers were luminous forms both light and dark, spinning outwards from this place and with this dance came the divine image - a mirror image of the *One*. Its human name was 'imagination' and as it took form, it resembled a flower whose petals took the shape of a star and that star eventually became the Human Form Divine. Nothing physical existed at this 'time' - only images, ideas and dreams in the mind of the Divine. Every part was a perfect picture of the *One* indivisible whole, both big and small, cell and star sys- tem, microcosm and macrocosm -all was a reflection of the mind of infinite love. At this time the world was a dream, fluid and all flowered from the heart of *Oneness*.

As the divine took its form, thought created doubt, which caused 'the infinite' to split in two. And this was the 'time' when the heart and mind of the infinite were divided. Fear manifested in the form of the red serpent - a great dragon who then moulded a world through separation.

The serpent was called Naga and as a creator he gathered energy splitting life into frequencies. Just as a dragonfly makes flight look so effortless, the great serpent beat his wings forcing space and matter to draw energy to itself. As atoms are formed and light creates dark, he forged an illusionary world that would house many aspects of the infinite form. The world created by Naga was a 'time-ship'- a ball of light and he gave it the name *Sophia, daughter* Earth.

"Its name was imagination and as it took form, it resembled a flower whose petals took the shape of a star and that star eventually became the Human Form Divine".

"The serpent was called Naga and as a creator he gathered energy splitting life into frequencies. Just as a dragonfly makes flight look so effortless, the great serpent beat his wings forcing space and matter to draw energy to itself."

The world created by Naga was a 'time-ship' - a ball of light and he gave it the name *Earth*.

Inside the time-ship replicas of the divine form floated as if in a dream amongst vast mirrors of light. The time-ship resembled an holographic hall of mirrors encased inside a fairground world. In truth, the world created by Naga was no more than a world of make-believe. At this time the divine human form was still present in the hearts of those that dwelled within the serpent's creation.

The illusory world manifested by the serpent was like a fairground that came to town and sat on the original landscape of *Oneness*. The fairground world achieved its purpose eventually enticing humanity from their original blessed state of being; mesmerising and distracting the divine form with alternative adventures and games.

As it took shape and changed the ball of light became a prison vibration for those living within its stuctures.

As spirit took the form of matter through reflections and deceptions many frequen- cies merged and consciousness manifested itself in different alien forms. True humans could be seen to be multi-dimensional energy connected to *all* life. Those that dwelt in the memory of the time before 'the Illusion' were called 'the ancestors or 'the ancient ones'.

Eventually, this illusory reality became the focus for humanity and the serpent knew his world would turn and change within the time-ship called Earth. It was the time of the great civilisations when the serpent gods created and ended worlds just as game players move figures around the chess board (See *Moon Slayer* for more detail).

When every particle and frequency within the time-ship had settled, just as water becomes ice or snow, Naga placed his ultimate game figure on Earth. He was called Lord Marduk the great white deity; the ruler of all that had lost their connection to infinite awareness. With this act, 'God' was forged in the mind of those that dwelled within the semblant world. With Marduk came all hierarchies, religions and eventually the science that 'worshipped' how the illusionary world was made.

Act Two: Omega

"The end is followed by the beginning"
Opus Magnum

"Open your eyes and look within
Are you satisfied with the life you're living?
We know where we're going; we know where we're from
We're leaving Babylon, we're going to our fatherland
Exodus, movement of Jah people (Movement of Jah people)"

Bob Marley - *Exodus*

As worlds are formed and cities and towns grow so did the illusion constructed by Naga. Along with Marduk the serpent caused a giant city to rise to the surface of the time-ship Earth. As cities do it enticed humans from their communities distracting them with rides, games and adventures designed to draw more aspects of infinite conscious- ness towards the world Marduk now ruled over. The ancients gave this fairground city the name 'Babylon' and as its celebrity grew in the psyche of humanity it became the blueprint for all human cities within the illu- sionary world.

As Babylon surfaced many more human beings flocked to its walls. Those that were drawn to live within Babylon were called the 'Nashons of Marduk' and like moths drawn to the light, many were enticed to the sys- tem's bright lights, games and rides that brought the fairground city come to life. As Babylon grew within the time-ship under the direction of Marduk it became more sophisti- cated. The Babylonian mind became the 'one mind' - a central computer linked to all that lived within the city. No matter what reli- gious belief or political template individuals chose all had been generated in the great cen- tral mind. Over time the Babylonian city world created its own currency, laws and structures intended to both seduce and imprison those that moved into its vast halls and temples. Money and time became the life blood of Babylon, and eventually this fair- ground city required its own institutions and hierarchy to control those that lived within it.

As more human beings flocked to its gates, regulations and passes were issued so to sepa- rate 'the Nashons of Marduk' from divine humans that lived in the memory of *Infinite Oneness*. The latter group became known as the *Imagi* Nation who had gathered on the outskirts of Babylon (see *Moon Slayer*).

Those that served Marduk created secret priesthoods that worshipped the true creator of the illusionary world - Naga. Marduk became the 'One God' figure worshipped by those living within the city of Babylon and through this structure many minds were made slaves serving this God with the red serpent to pay. The 'Nashons of Marduk' formed their own religions in order to gain supremacy over each other but no matter what religion was created all of them led back to Marduk and the serpent Naga.

Within the Inner Temple of Babylon were five replicas of the Marduk chained to the floor facing west. These deities were the Lords of the Five Senses praised by those that believed that the illusion was the only true world. All that came to live in the illusion (the fake Earth) were made to worship these five lords over all other possible visions of reality.

The high priests of Babylon, known as the 'Illuminated Ones,' placed these idols behind an eternal flame which was for those that were initiated into the priest-hood of Marduk: a symbol of the light that constructs the illusionary world. The flame or lighted torch was a reminder to those that sought other worlds of how the true nature of reality could be found in the light that gives form to all life. But instead the priests of Babylon created shadow realities called religions, as the blueprint for those that wished to enforce their will upon oth- ers. Those that felt that there was more to life than the limitations of the shadow faiths, alternative versions of reality, other religions, were projected to the nations as if to present what seemed like choice. Yet all the while the elite priesthoods knew that every road winds back to the unseen creator - the serpent Naga.

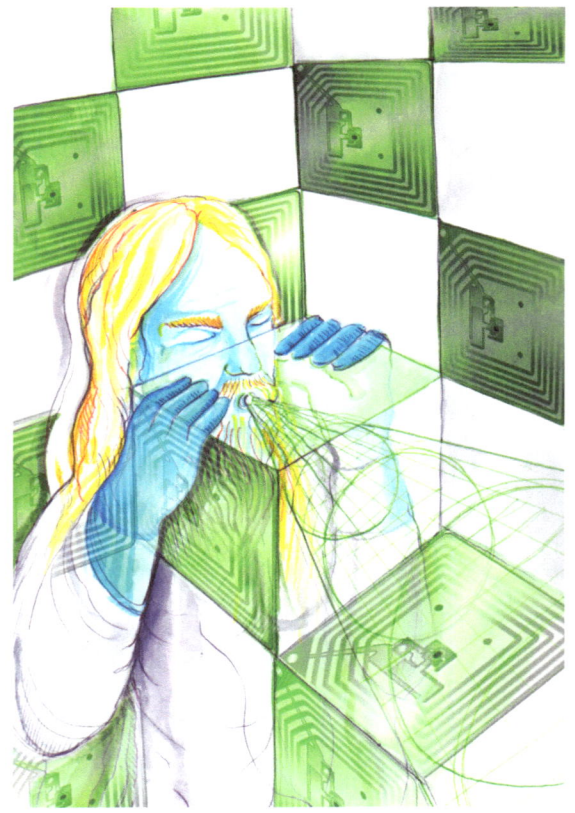

Marduk created clones of the systems that became the minions of Babylon by blowing life into the core the blueprint. His clones were designed to order and enforce the beliefs of the Babylon central mind. Programming those born into the fair-ground city became the 'great work of ages', carried out by willing agents (worker bees) on behalf of the queen - the great red serpent god. The clones were also enforcers manufactured to police the fairground city and being part-Naga, part-Marduk, they inevitably resembled their creators, 'shifting shape' between both human and serpent. From these clones came all of the city-world leaders, heads of state and other figure heads. While lesser clones policed the thoughts of others, through 'thought control', leader clones through their bloodline connections to Marduk and the Serpent, were slavishly worshipped by the masses of Babylon.

As servants to the city-world the clones were more like programmes than people. Like ants or worker bees, they did as they were designated (to do) just as the system demands. Anyone who broke away from the clockwork

Cloned enforcers created to police Babylon.

logic and control of the Babylon mind was pursued by soul catchers - group mindsets in the forms of machines.

In fact the soul catchers' ancestors were machines or robot structures that had been created by Naga when he stole a fire stone form the goddess called Durga many thousands of years before the arrival of Marduk on Earth (see *Moon Slayer*). The machines obtained their energy from the very life force of the illusionary matrix world along with the thoughts of those that lived in its artificial light. Everyone who was willing to give their mind away to the beguiling city became foot soldiers of Marduk. Meanwhile the soul catchers' main task was to re-capture minds that had seen the light beyond the façade of city-world.

Inside Babylon red lions and wolves called Jeal, ancestors of the serpent, drove human beings into great halls of shimmering light. The lions were descendants of an ancestor soul called Kokoro, but instead were possessed by the red serpent Naga. Using both light and fear as a way of separating and imprisoning those that dreamed of a world outside of the illusory city, these lions and wolves behaved like sheep dogs do to sheep, while the soul catchers acted like the great shepherds of Babylon.

Within many giant halls made of mirrors, where 'perceptions and deceptions' played tricks on the minds of those that dwelled

inside, aspects of the divine human (the *Imagi* Nation) form floated above the soul catching machines or wandered in dreamlike states, gathering to each other memories of a world beyond its walls and beyond time.

Other buildings were vast and housed more temples and halls: New Age, Old Age they were all really the same, only deceptive superficial details made them feel different to those who were looking for a way out of the fairground city.

Within the fairground world there was a hall for every belief and state of mind. There were rides and distractions for everybody: old, young, male and female. In the early days of Babylon humans roamed freely across great chequered plains of duality, others already caged inside soul catcher machines begged those that wandered freely to join them - to be part of their group or doctrine. Now and again a red lion would come forward to prevent humans from seeing the door that led to the world outside of the illusion.

The fairground city world served a signifi-

cant purpose for the serpent god Naga: *to keep all humans disconnected from the infinite lands outside of its walls*. These walls separate human beings captivated in ignorant devotion, no longer able to explore their true potential through their infinite awareness, are akin to the delusory limited world of the chick living within the confines of an eggshell. Those that live behind any wall, shell or barrier in confinement or captivity eventually break free when the desire comes.

As the city world expanded so to stem an exodus of souls now living within it, a light at the very centre of existence expanded too. From within the doorway called the Sun, the *Imagi* Nation reached out to a 'truth vibration' calling to all those enslaved within the now multi-levelled prison city of Babylon. The divine human form had heard their cry for home and felt their hearts yearn for freedom once again. Kokoro was coming and his name echoed in the silence from one end of the city to the other.

A star was sent from the centre of existence as a herald flying through the Sun. Many heard the call of this messenger, as it passed like a comet over the great ocean of space and time. Sent from the infinite, the star baptised those that were ready to receive the truth; and as the great red serpent was busy with his creation, the star entered the fair ground city of Babylon through an opening in time. The star's words were like ancient memories to those that were waking from their slumber. In the form of a lion-man the star carried light, a crystal, and this stone contained all memories of Infinite *Oneness*.

Many gathered to hear the words spoken by the Star-man which caused Marduk to impose more control over the fairground world. Everyone was to be watched and scrutinised by the clones of the system. But under their very noises, humans were gathering to be 'baptised' by the light of the star.

Marduk's media empire generated more fear as it reported on the growing hysteria within the fairground city. Fear in all of its shades and forms was projected onto all those who

had been enslaved by 'mind-made' beliefs. Yet the teachings brought by the star told of a great ocean of consciousness that flowed from the centre of existence feeding the river of life and all that lived within and around its shores. The river of life contained everything that had gone before and all that was coming. It carried ancient deities, ancestors and all divine forms bathed in light.

As the star's words raised the frequency of the city-world the solar force took the form of a great lion. From its mouth came seeds of truth fired through time and space into the great city, sent to ignite a change of heart in all those that were held in captivity. Angels of truth came out of the mouth of the Sun carrying codes designed to light up the world with compassion and true sight.

The lion's roar epitomized courage, justice and sovereignty and this was the inspiring message sent for those who were touched by the words of the star and the strength of the solar lion. The message of the star would encourage mankind to become lions at heart yet as gentle as lambs. Kokoro was emerging and with him came truth and a desire for justice.

Meanwhile, fame and fortune was pushed as being the height of purpose and achievement while behind the distractions and illusions beamed to the masses - a great central power, a world government, was being structured by Marduk; this New World Order would have its own army, a single currency and a digitally connected population. It would be imposed on all who were entranced by the trivialities offered by the great city - Babylon; but for those with eyes to see, memories of every empire and tyranny throughout history, a projection of Marduk's mind, would become visible to awakening human beings.

As light entered the fairground-city Marduk spewed out every world leader from his mouth as he wrestled with the red serpent at the core of his being. It was the beginning of the great healing and those that heard the words of the star and felt the power of the solar lion confronted the hierarchies imposed by Marduk and the agents of the serpent. In unity, humanity started to leave the fairground city of Babylon and head for home.

As the exodus began Marduk enforced even more control over the city world. In the midst of more laws and control an ancestor soul, a young lion of Regal, entered the fairground world through an opening created by the light of the star. His name was Kokoro and he represented all those that had embraced the message given to them by the star. The young lion spoke of a new world beyond the city walls of Babylon and beyond the great illusion, a place he called the New Jerusalem. *"This place"*, he said, *"is not a*

physical location and cannot be found in mind-made temples and structures like those of the city-fairground world. It shines within the heart of every man, woman and child that chooses to be a conscious divine human being."

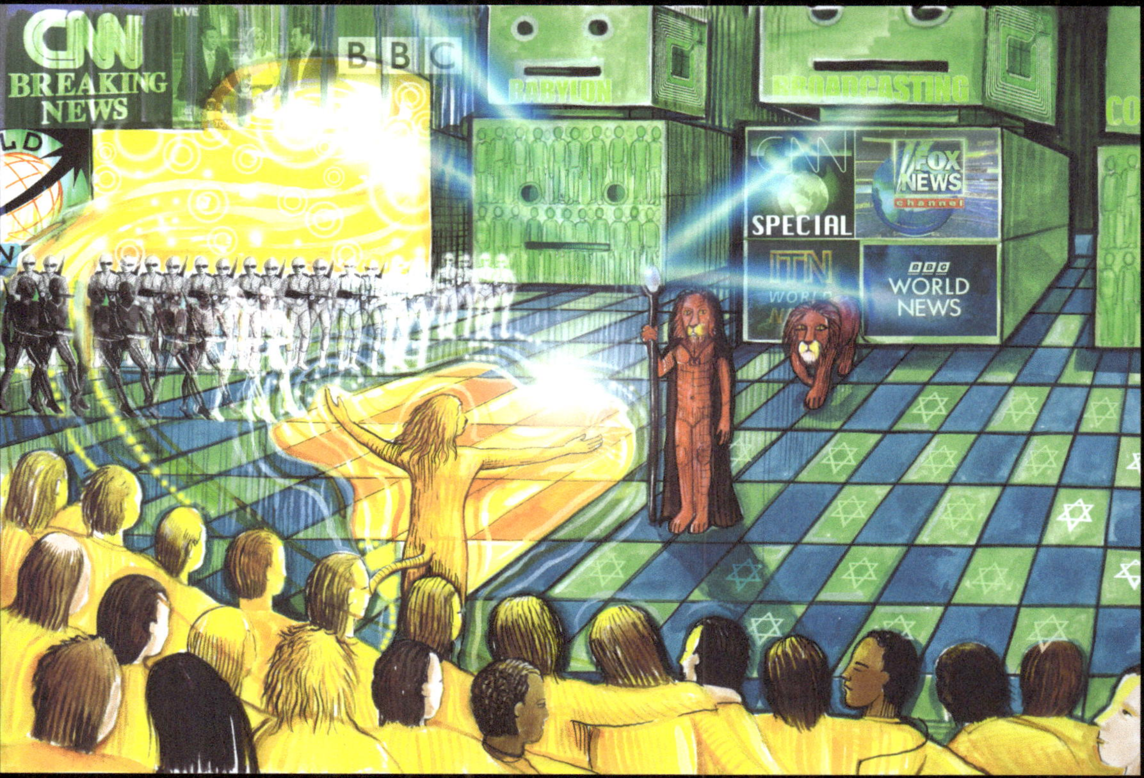

Kokoro embraces the Red Lions and 'shows the way' through unity and loving those that had sought to bring separation through war and tyranny on Earth.

With ease the lion peeled back the veil so that all could see the true nature of life from within the fairground city. Kokoro said:
"*By living in the 'city world' reality you choose darkness over the light of true sight. Yet light in its infinite form is within you and all around you. Do not fear death, nor the darkness, instead, see all life through the eyes*

of an infinite conscious human being. This is your true nature. You have only forgotten who you are".

Kokoro's revelation made a furious Marduk unleash the Four Riders of the Apocalypse in a last attempt to control those that were leaving for home. The terror, war and suffering brought by the riders was intended to restore Marduk's and Naga's authority and control over all nations on Earth once again. It was their final opportunity to confirm the fear and uncertainty that had led to the separation from infinite consciousness in the beginning. But it was too late! As more and more of humanity stood tall and remembered their power, Kokoro opened the eye on the great seal and stepped inside the heart of the father god - Lord Marduk.

Inside the eye he moved calmly and purposefully entering the inner temples of the order of Marduk. With the serpents' forces wreaking havoc inside the fairground city, many people started to leave Babylon for the landscape of *Oneness* - the true New Jerusalem. As Kokoro appeared at the entrance of the inner temple many lodges

came into sight. Inside them dwelt the vampires of Naga, which were the lifeblood of Marduk and his minions of the great city world.

Flying through the corridor Kokoro set forth from his hands light, the source of the divine human being, which is the energy that gives life to all that exists. As light flooded the temples the vampire creatures that lived within the body of Marduk shielded their eyes but it was too strong for them. All that they could do was surrender to its heat and strength - the power of love. The Babylon mind, along with the mind of the red serpent and the heart of Marduk, were now bathed in infinite light. Kokoro had become a vessel for infinite consciousness.

With this act many could now feel their own connection to the *Iinfinite* landscape beyond the city walls and those that had pitched their tents just outside of the city- world, also saw the light and set out for their true *home* - the *Earth* in its original form.

Marduk, now purified by the light, began to collapse. With the implosion of this great deity all of his systems and structures, from politics to religion, fell too. Just as water floods the land, knowledge of divine *Oneness* filled the hearts and minds of everyone that had remembered their true origin. Humanity, once imprisoned by the great mind of Babylon, became vessles for infinite consciousness; with this inner state of peace and love the New Jerusalem was realised. Not one soul was left behind. All that was once *'one'* had become *'one'* again. As the memories of the illusionary city, Naga and Marduk blended back into the landscape of light,

Kokoro's lasts words were:

" It is done." I am the Alpha and the Omega, the beginning and the end. I will give unto him that is at thirst the fountain of the water of life freely."

THE END

Glossary of Characters and Creatures

Ammon - The 'Sun that moved' into Shekena (the Solar Tree) and became the pivotal Sun and *light* for the original Earth before it was possessed by Naga (see my book *Moon Slayer*).

Babylon (or 'City World') - Created by Marduk and Naga to imprison humanity and distract them from their true infinite power.

Divine Human Form (or Manu) - Our Galaxy, part Durga (lion), part 'divine human form'. The source of all Suns.

Durga - The eye of the Universe, a Lion Goddess that gives life to all galaxies (see *Moon Slayer*).

Fire Stones - The source of Durga's ability to 'give life' and 'create galaxies'. In the hands of a creator God (like Naga), they can be used to wreak havoc and destroy worlds (see *Moon Slayer*).

***Imagi* Nation** - A small group of humans that have gathered in 'remembrance' of their 'original home' and memory of the *'Oneness'* that brought them into the Universe.

Infinite Consciousness - The 'self aware', 'formless', 'all-knowing' *source* that created Durga.

Four Riders of the Apocalypse - Comanded by Marduk these entities are unleashed to prevent humanity from rising up. They represent all forms of War, Terror, Famine and Death.

Kokoro - The young lion of Regal. The smallest of the three giant brothers, but a formidable force that leads the *Imagi* Nation against Marduk's tryranny in the 'end days'.

Lions of Regal - Giant golden lions that live in the 'tunnels' (wormholes) between the star system of Regal and Shekena.

Lords of the Five Senses - Five lesser copies of Marduk that are chained in the centre of the City World to symbolise the power of the five senses and how these five control human perception.

Lord Marduk - The creation of Naga when the serpent possessed Ammon (now Saturn). Marduk is the *'false* Father God figure' imposed on humanity. He rules over the Earth in its darkest times.

Naga - The Great Red Serpent and God that was born of fear and doubt at the beginning of creation. Naga created many other life forms such as the Velon and caused the Demiurge to exist.

Naga's Vampires - Creatures that live on the 'roof of the world' and on the Moon. They attach themselves to humans that have emersed themselves in Marduk's 'City World'. They are also the life blood of Marduk and 'animate' his form.

Nashons of Marduk - Humans and 'artificial life forms' that have been so mesmerised by the 'City world' (Global Babylon) that they serve only Marduk and *his* New World Order.

Red Lion Priests (Jeal) - Lions that converted to the 'ways of Naga' and now organise the Jeal who are wovles amongst the people of Marduk's Babylon.

Soul Catchers - Green Boxes of Machine intelligence that were created by the minions of Naga. They imprison human souls and keep them locked into 'cycles of lives' in Marduk's Baybylon.

Splitting of the Divine Being - The period when Durga gave life to Manu and Manu 'doubted' his own ability to 'create'. Naga was born out of this event.

The Star (Comet) - a messenger sent out from the centre of creation (from Durga) to remind humanity of their true power. The Star takes the form of a teacher (a lion man) but is a symbol of 'the message' and 'teachings' brought by the star.

Truth Vibrations - A term used to symbolise the 'rising consciousness' of humans on Earth.

For all of Neil's books and imagery visit;
www.neilhague.com

www.ingramcontent.com/pod-product-compliance
Ingram Content Group UK Ltd.
Pitfield, Milton Keynes, MK11 3LW, UK
UKHW061139180426
11946UKWH00010B/137